THE LIBRARY

OF ILLUMINATED MANUSCRIPTS

edited by Walter Oakeshott

The

Douce Apocalypse

THE LIBRARY OF ILLUMINATED MANUSCRIPTS

edited by Walter Oakeshott

THE DOUCE APOCALYPSE

with an introduction and notes
by

A. G. and W. O. HASSALL

NEW YORK : THOMAS YOSELOFF

JM

Introduction

The Douce Apocalypse is a picture-book of outstanding beauty illustrating in detail the Book of Revelation of St. John the Divine. In general the familiar words of the Authorized Version are a sufficient explanation for each scene represented. There are however some exceptions, as on p. 27; for in *Revelation* viii, 13 the English translation has 'an angel flying through the midst of heaven', but the *Vulgate* (here illustrated) has an eagle not an angel.

The Douce Apocalypse begins with a translation into Anglo-Norman. Apart from the opening page[1] this part of the manuscript is a text, not a picture-book. This is followed by a second part which once consisted of one hundred pictured pages. Of these ninety-seven survive, for collation[2] shows that the three pages are missing which should have illustrated *Revelation* iv, 1 to v, 1; v, 8–14; and xiv, 6–8. On each page there is a panel containing a picture. Under this panel there is the text which it illustrates, handsomely written in Latin. This is occasionally amplified in the form of a popular commentary written by Berengaudus[3] in the ninth century. This commentary is summarized in the *Glossa Ordinaria* and explains *Revelation* allegorically in terms of the early Church. It lacks accordingly such references to current affairs as Alexander of Bremen[4] introduced in 1232, references inspired by the example of Joachim da Fiore,[5] when he found in the visions of St. John prophecies of the Crusades, of the coming of the Friars, and of the advent of Antichrist and the last era of the world in 1260.

The second part of the Douce Apocalypse is a true picture-book of the type which inspired the block books of the fifteenth century, and the text is so subordinate to the pictures that the scribe sometimes leaves a sentence unfinished or repeated in order to keep all the writing on a page relevant to the picture while fairly filling the allotted space.

Each page is $12\frac{1}{4}$ in. high and $8\frac{1}{2}$ in. wide. The Latin text in the second part of the manu-script occupies the lower half of each page. The panels containing pictures occupy the upper halves and measure $4\frac{3}{8}$ in. high by $5\frac{3}{4}$ in. wide. This is smaller than the panels in the fine Apocalypse at Trinity College, Dublin,[6] which differ also from ours in having a vertical instead of a horizontal format and in having geometrically shaped inner frames. The general effect is of course very different from those Apocalypses, executed about the same time, with two panels on each page and no separate text. The Douce manuscript is not one of those which are preceded by the Life of St. John, like that recently in the Dyson Perrins collection;[7] nor does it contain the four miracles wrought by Antichrist which are inserted in chapter 11 in manuscripts of what Delisle and Meyer call the 'first family';[8] nor is it one of those in which the illustrations are tinted outline drawings.[9]

The script looks like the work of a single scribe. It is carefully arranged in double columns of text written in large letters, while the commentary is written with letters half the size (or occasionally *vice versa* if good spacing rather than consistency suggests such a reversal). The ruling is elaborate, with an external frame of double line dividing the columns and with lines ruled between all the lines of the text of whatever size. The text, like some of the pictures, was left unfinished, for spaces were left for initials on every page though only two of these initials were ever inserted. Scribal blunders occur but were left uncorrected. Thus on the last page John, instead of Jesus, is called the root of David. The script is as handsome an example as one could wish of the pointed Gothic handwriting which came in with the pointed arches of thirteenth-century architecture to supersede the rounded style of Romanesque taste (Plate 12), and which lasted until Renaissance scholars imitated Roman models in Italy in the fifteenth century.

A picture of Henry III's son and successor the Lord Edward with his wife, Eleanor, before they became king and queen, occurs on the first page of the first part of the manuscript which suggests that the first owners were the royal pair. If, however, E. B. W. Nicholson's interpretation of a pen-trial on fol. 5 of the first part is valid, the Douce Apocalypse passed into monastic ownership, although the use of Anglo-Norman suggests that it was meant to belong to a layman. An ornate binding of about 1600 suggests that the book went to an Oxford binder.

It is not known who owned the manuscript until it came into the possession of William Wilson, Esq., F.S.A., of the Minories on whose death it was sold among his 'Pictures, drawings, prints, books or prints, trinkets and curiosities' by Messrs. Christie and Manson on 1 February 1833. Mr. N. R. Ker[10] found a catalogue of the sale in the Bodleian library (Mus. Bibl. III 4° 37) in which, against the entry 'The REVELATIONS OF ST. JOHN, a curious early manuscript on vellum, with ninety-seven large illuminations, in ancient binding', there is a marginal note in the handwriting of Francis Douce: 'I afterwards bought this fine MS. of Thorpe.' The purchaser kept a diary of antiquarian purchases and in it he wrote under February 1833: 'Beautiful MS. Revelations (Wilsons), of Thorpe.'[11] Douce (1757–1834) was keeper of manuscripts in the British Museum. He quarrelled with the trustees, built up a fine collection of manuscripts, partly with money inherited from the sculptor Nollekens, and left his books and manuscripts to the Bodleian Library. There this Apocalypse is called MS. Douce 180.

M. R. James was convinced that the Douce Apocalypse was executed at Canterbury.[12] This was because it was one of a group of seven illustrated English Apocalypses in which certain islands are shown with their names in the first Apocalypse picture. Of these one (MS. Lambeth 209) is connected with St. Augustine's Canterbury and another (once MS. Yates Thompson 55) is its sister. His other reason was that 'high authorities have seen French influence in it and Canterbury is a place where French influence was strong: we see it not only in the fabric of the cathedral but in its glass, which is of a date not greatly earlier than our MS.'[13] Miss O. E. Saunders remarked that no known Canterbury work was so good, but on the basis of these suggestions made by a great scholar, the name of Canterbury has become indelibly associated with the Douce Apocalypse and writers about it have echoed, and will doubtless continue to re-echo, this opinion, for it is enshrined in the facsimile edition to which they will always turn. It must be clearly understood that it is the conjecture of a modern scholar who had, perforce, little evidence on which to base this particular theory. More probable, however, is the belief of Miss O. E. Saunders that the work is that of the Court school. The whole atmo-sphere is courtly, chivalrous and romantic with worldly colour and the recurrence of such significant little details as a fondness for fashionable vair linings (pp. 36, 37, 48, 49, 50, 52 and 53). Dr. E. G. Millar,[14] Professor Tristram[15] and Professor Wormald[16] have alike commented on its similarity with the famous Westminster panel[17] while the careful shading of the figures and severe folds of the drapery have been noted as precursors of late thirteenth-century court work in the Tenison and Arundel Psalters. This contrasts with the more spiritual atmo-sphere in the Lambeth Apocalypse.

*   *   *   *

The names of both scribe and artist are unknown; but they ranked among the most accom-plished masters of their arts in the thirteenth century. That century was the great period of Gothic art in Northern Europe. It gave us not only much of the best of Westminster Abbey, but, during the reigns of Henry III of England and of his brother-in-law St. Louis of France, many great cathedrals and supreme works of sculpture were created on both sides of the Channel. These, and stained glass, are more widely known than the wonderful illuminated manuscripts, notably Bibles and parts of Bibles, of which the glories are largely hidden. The names of the artists are seldom recorded, though work produced in the previous generation by William de Brailes and Matthew Paris has been identified.

*   *   *   *

No colophon gives a date for the production of this manuscript. Sir Sydney Cockerell pointed out that the arms borne by the (uncrowned) figures of the Lord Edward and Eleanor of Castile are those used by them between 1254 and 1272. It is absurd to assign a narrowly defined date on grounds of script or artistic style; for a man of established repute entrusted with work for the royal family might use a single style for several decades and formal scripts do not change fast. The *Summary Catalogue of Western Manuscripts in the Bodleian Library* (no. 21754) assigns it to the last quarter of the thirteenth century. The *Palaeographical Society* ii, 77 is also doubtless too late in dating it about 1280; but E. B. W. Nicholson was excessively precise when he was unable to doubt that the volume was illuminated in '1263-5—probably between April 1264 and June 1265'.

Nicholson's precise dating was based on a belief that some of the arms in the battle scenes allude to Simon de Montfort and Gilbert de Clare. They are ranged, as the Lord Edward would have expected, among the host of Satan, which is not where a Benedictine monk filled with the prejudices of a Matthew Paris in favour of 'Earl Simon the righteous', that worker of miracles, would have placed him. It was, however, in line with the application to England by Pope Urban IV in condemning baronial conspiracies on 23 August 1263 of the passage in *Job* i, 12, 19: 'Satan went forth from the presence of the Lord . . . and, behold, there came a great wind from the wilderness, and smote' the Kingdom of England, and the Register of Clement IV testifies to the great bitterness of that Pope in 1265 against Simon de Montfort. M. R. James thought the arms were of no significance and pointed out that anyhow tricks had been played with the colours. In fact, as the note on p. 31 suggests, the changes of the colours

7

may be extraordinarily significant. To clinch his argument James cites as 'a plain case of imaginative fancy' the attribution on pp. 87 and 80 of three frogs as arms to Satan. But this emblem is most apposite and is explained in a passage illustrated in this and many other Apocalypse manuscripts and in the tapestry Apocalypse at Angers. St. John 'saw three unclean spirits like frogs come out of the mouth of the dragon, and out of the mouth of the beast, and out of the false prophet. For they are the spirits of devils, working miracles, which go forth unto the Kings of the earth' (*Revelation* xvi, 13, 14). The *Vulgate* is clearer still and runs 'Sunt enim spiritus daemoniorum facientes signa'. *Signa* means 'miracles' to priests, but to knights it means badges of identification such as the *signum* under which Constantine was bidden to conquer when, according to Lactantius, he marked the *signum dei* on his shields. This is the meaning of the word 'sign' in the English Legendary of 1290 when it is borne on a banner and it is thus used on p. 19 of the Douce Apocalypse. In *Flores Historiarum* we find that the Royalists at the final defeat of Simon de Montfort by The Lord Edward in 1265 were 'rubeo signo in brachiis ambobus cruce signati'. The meaning of frogs used as a sign is suggested by St. Augustine's comparison of frogs to vain and wordy heretics. The *Glossa Ordinaria* explains that the croaking of frogs in sloughs disturbs the peace, and Nicolas de Lyra later particularized this croaking as coming from the mouths of Saracen leaders. The newly introduced vizors of thirteenth-century armour made such marks of identification necessary on the shields of knights; and even in our literate generation a man's mark is called his *signature*, every inn has its sign, and emblems such as a swastika or a hammer and sickle have certain significances which are more obvious than others. In the third quarter of the thirteenth century heraldry was a thoroughly modern and interesting art and science of obvious beauty, utility and meaning. All the windows of the King's Great Chamber at the Tower and at the King's Chamber at Winchester were decorated between 1240 and 1265 with the King's arms. Armorial glass was ordered with the king's shield and that of the *late* Count of Provence for Rochester Castle in 1247 and more was ordered for the palace at Havering-atte-Bower in 1251 and again in 1268. It is hard to believe that Montfort's lion with a forked tail would have seemed so insignificant to the Lord Edward as it does to M. R. James; but after Montfort fell at Evesham in 1265 those arms would, in spite of E. B. W. Nicholson, have remained significant. It need not, therefore, be assumed that this picture was made earlier.

* * * *

Henry III gave opportunities to several scores of English artists in his palaces and castles and at Westminster. He was devoted to the memory of St. Edward the Confessor, the builder of Westminster Abbey. He had more paintings made of his legend than of any subject except the Virgin and Child and the Crucifixion, he chose him as his patron saint, and after him he named his heir, later Edward I. A Court School of painters arose, recruited throughout the land and inspired by the king's cultural contacts with the courts of France and Norway. This Court School was centred on the Palace and the Abbey of Westminster but Professor Tristram has pointed out that royal generosity disseminated the artistic products of London and Westminster as gifts throughout his realm. Important schools at St. Albans and Canterbury had employed lay painters but had remained monastic centres. The Westminster school had the court for its inspiration and its influence in the second half of the century was dominant. The wall paintings which it produced are largely destroyed but in the Westminster panel we have a surviving masterpiece.

A false impression may be conjured up by speaking of the 'English Court'. The English language was not the language of the King of England, and if the ancestry of Edward I is traced back as far as 1100 it is found to include only one English ancestor, St. Margaret, Queen of Scotland. Dominating, and unpopular, elements in the court of Henry III were the French relations of his French mother and of his French Queen. National patriotism was still an unknown concept and European upper-class society had a real unity; indeed Henry III of England, Louis IX of France, Charles of Anjou, and Richard Earl of Cornwall, the King of the Romans, were all brothers-in-law through marriage to the daughters of Raymond Berenger, Count of Provence. Perhaps even more significant of the unreality of nationality in the thirteenth century is the career of another of Henry III's brothers-in-law, Simon de Mont-fort. Simon, the leader of 'national' resistance to royal extravagance was invited by the French nobles to be seneschal of France in 1252 and to take a leading part in the regency of France. Simon came of very important French ancestry and readers of *Vanity Fair* will be impressed by the fact that his mother was a Montmorency. Henry III's grandfather, though king of England, had ruled more of France than had the French King himself, for his southern frontier had been on the Pyrenees. Among prominent people, whose lives and ancestry are well documented, the strands of English and French influence are intimately intertwined. 'Now', declares *La Estoire de Seint Aedward le Rei* in praise of Henry III, 'are King, now are barons, and the kingdom of a common blood of England and Normandy.' We know nothing about the detailed heredity and environment, movements and contacts of artists who are little more than names to us; few exactly dated and localized examples of their products remain and it is rather fruitless to dis-tinguish English and French elements. The very surname of the best known and most English artist is Paris. His monastery of St. Albans lay on an important road and often housed members of the court with all their foreign background; and Paris himself certainly visited not only Westminster but even Norway. To call the style of the Douce Apocalypse English or French is a subjective judgement. Nationalism often causes writers to claim great artists for their own countries and it is consoling to see Delisle and Meyer in *L'Apocalypse en Français au xiiie siècle* (Société des anciens textes français) call the book English, while the *Palaeographical Society* (ii, 77) and the *Summary Catalogue of Western Manuscripts in the Bodleian Library* do not hesitate to call it French. Miss Rickert states that the manuscript was possibly written in France and Sir Sidney Cockerel was never convinced that the illuminator was English. The Channel linked rather than divided the cultures of England and those of Northern France and Flanders. Even without the Norman Conquest the link would have been strong. In view of the continual coming and going which took place along the routes of Medieval Europe it is dangerous to assign to one side of the Channel, merely on grounds of appearance, what may have in fact been brought from the other or have been produced by someone who shared, with every one

9

else of the time, close links with the other. It is, however, an undisputed fact that the inscriptions on scrolls in certain pictures in the Douce Apocalypse are written in the French of England. If the work of production did not actually take place at Westminster it is, considering the destination of the book, highly probable that the artist was one of the many who enjoyed the patronage of Henry III and worked for the court. Such artists could come from as far afield as Italy, but the majority were born in various parts of England and some had connections with East Anglia. It was, however, a time when in any kind of art Parisian influences would be natural.

Illustrated Apocalypse manuscripts were especially characteristic of the Channel School in the thirteenth century, this characteristic being strongest north of the Channel and spreading elsewhere in time. The Lamb on Mount Sion (*Revelation* xiv) together with the symbols of the Four Evangelists occurs as early as the late fourth century in mosaic in St. Pudentiana at Rome. A series of images of the Apocalypse were brought back to England from Rome in 684 when Benedict Biscop had them transposed onto the walls of Wearmouth. The Eastern church produced no early Apocalypse illustrations since it did not recognize *Revelation* as canonical before the fourteenth century. Until Northumbria was ruined by the Danish invasions it was the greatest centre of light and learning in Europe. It was thence that Alcuin came to the court of Charlemagne and the paintings of Wearmouth may have stirred imitation elsewhere. Be that as it may, eighth- or ninth-century manuscripts at Trier and Cambrai preserve series of over seventy Apocalypse pictures and equally long series occur in Spanish manuscripts of the Commentary on the Apocalypse written by Beatus[18] who died in 798. A particularly fine Apocalypse with fifty pictures was produced at Reichenau about 1100 and is now at Bamberg.[19] There is, however, a sharp break in the tradition, followed in the thirteenth century by a revival, which is strongest in England, its place of origin, and on which earlier influences are slight.

*   *   *   *

At least ninety-three manuscripts survive which were produced in the thirteenth, fourteenth and fifteenth centuries to illustrate the Apocalypse.[20] These have been divided into groups, according to differences of content by Delisle, and according to differences of form by M. R. James. These groupings do not coincide with one another. Miss O. E. Saunders[21] has devoted eleven plates to illustrating the artistic groups of English Apocalypses, for it is in England that the greater and better part of these manuscripts was produced. She reproduces four examples assigned to St. Albans, two to Canterbury, two to East Anglia, and two, of which one is the Douce Apocalypse and one a manuscript in Paris, which she thinks were by Court artists.

It would be interesting to know why the Channel School produced scores of illustrated Apocalypses in the thirteenth century. Spectacular events like the murder of St. Thomas Becket by Henry II, the struggle against the followers of Mahomet, the crusade against the heretics of Toulouse, or the strife between Pope and Emperor were terrific happenings which might lend an added interest to the Apocalypse; but then many other generations have witnessed events which might seem to herald the end of the world. Whether it was a symptom or a cause, or both, a popular vernacular translation into Norman French of *Revelation* appeared in the late twelfth century about the time when Joachim da Fiore propounded his interpretation of the book to King Richard I. This translation was not only much copied but became the basis in the fourteenth century for a further translation, into English, and with the possible exception of the Psalms this was the first book of the Bible to appear in Middle English. If the Norman French translation were studied by an artist, or a patron of artists, or by a preacher interested in visual aids, it is not surprising that the idea of a further translation into visual terms was born, for pictures on the walls of churches were loved in an illiterate age, and a book could display more pictures than the Doom which filled a chancel arch.

The spread of preaching with the advent of the Friars may have widened and deepened lay interest in the subject and Friars are portrayed on pp. 36–8 as well as in at least three other Apocalypse manuscripts, including the Trinity College Apocalypse which is held to antedate the others, though the architectural details contradict this. Franciscans were especially interested in the Apocalypse. Whether or not a Franciscan made a French translation of Berengaudus, a companion of St. Francis (perhaps significantly, an Englishman) was interested in Apocalypse pictures;[22] and in the late thirteenth century a Franciscan interpretation of the Apocalypse assigns an important place as the 'First Resurrection' to the advent of the Dominicans and the Franciscans.[23] In St. Bonaventura's official Life of St. Francis, St. Francis is seen as an angel of the Apocalypse; and he is accordingly portrayed as an angel of mercy warning the Winds not to complete the destruction until the elect should be gathered, in a series of Apocalypse frescoes in the Upper Church at Assisi.[24] The English court respected the Franciscans. Henry III was a founder of Franciscan convents and a correspondent of Adam Marsh, and his queen had a friar in her household.[25]

For whatever causes then, these manuscripts began to be produced, containing wide selections from a range of nearly one hundred different subjects. All of them have a family likeness. They contain delicate and charming drawing, striking colours, plain backgrounds, tall, thin, typically Early Gothic figures for St. John and the Angels and grotesque gargoyle-like forms for the hosts of darkness. Fashionable art of any age has a coherence which need not necessarily be traced to a single source. It may be that the thirteenth-century Apocalypses have a common origin traceable to the scriptorium of St. Albans. M. R. James believed that the earliest of the thirteenth-century illustrated Apocalypses was one produced about 1230 (or perhaps rather about 1250) and now at Trinity College Dublin, but Sir S. Cockerell could not agree that it was produced where James believed. In any case the careful division into groups which James devised might suggest the conclusion that the Apocalypses do not owe their similarities to a common archetype, but rather to the fact that a common theme is being illustrated by the artists of one generation working in a common artistic and social climate. The precise story of the genesis of thirteenth-century Apocalypses is thus unknown and perhaps unknowable.

*　　*　　*　　*

The pictures in the Douce Apocalypse have all been described by M. R. James. They were all reproduced, though mostly in black and white only, by the Oxford University Printer for presentation to the Roxburghe Club by C. H. St. John Hornby in 1922. Two coloured

35-mm. filmstrips, unfortunately incomplete, but containing supplementary matter from other illustrated Apocalypses at Oxford, have been published by Nicolette Grey (Jacob's Ladder Filmstrips) and the Bodleian Library has also issued a filmstrip and 2 in. by 2 in. coloured slides. There has never been a complete colour reproduction and the present book contains more such reproductions than all those elsewhere available other than in the form of film.

The importance of colour in the study should be stressed, and stressed apart from aesthetic questions or even symbolism, on the score of simple understanding of what the artist meant to portray. Thus M. R. James, working from a black-and-white photograph and from his in-grained knowledge of the words of the *Book of Revelation* sees on p. 2 St. John with his book on his knee. In fact, the formless smudge on the knee of the saint is only an offset printed from the colour of the opposite page at some time when the manuscript was temporarily damp. The saint has picked up his pen-knife, but has not yet seized the book which, ready bound, with ruled margins but no lines or text, he takes up later (pp. 5–10, 32–3 and 97). Just as, in the numerous buildings here shown, there occurs, among arches of Gothic design and those of sheer fantasy, the occasional presence of a round-headed Norman archway, so, in spite of the extraordinary freshness of the complexions with their rouge-daubed cheeks, the colours are muted and sombre compared with the bright colours which Miss O. E. Saunders remarks as typical in the Apocalypses of thirteenth-century England. A few light and pale colours accom-pany much grey and dark brown, with crimson, orange and deep blue. The murky effects, rather lacking in meretricious charm, are to be associated, not with the fairy-tale clear pinks and blues of later Gothic painting, but with the high solemnity of the Romanesque past. St. John's cloak (p. 9), an Indian red, sets the pattern of quiet harmonies grateful to the modern eye. This is only disturbed by a crude light emerald tint much in favour in medieval Bohemia and in the child's cheap paintbox of today. The same general quietness of hue distinguishes the Trinity College Apocalypse, where indeed the comparatively rare use of scarlet and the em-ployment of ranges of moss green and dull purple produces a still more sombre effect.

A colour reproduction of a number of pictures from the Douce Apocalypse is especially interesting for a study of illuminating technique. Professor Brieger is incorrect in suggesting that only a few of its pages are coloured but this manuscript ends with a number of uncoloured (quire 5, pp. 59–74) and half coloured (quires 6–7, pp. 75–97) pictures. These show the colourist's technique. After the draughtsman had made his drawings in bold sensitive lines gold was applied where needed. Then, instead of colour being laid on direct in the colours required as was often done elsewhere, pale flat washes were laid on in various colours and these were gradually painted over. Thus, to render flowers and leaves, light turquoise was applied and allowed to show through heavy overpaintings in the dark grey foregrounds of grass. In medieval book production the colourist was often not the same man as the draughtsman and was often much inferior in capability and understanding. In the Douce Apocalypse the colour plays an essential part in the finished work of art and may well have been painted on by the same man as did the drawing. He is occasionally capable of giving a striking atmospheric effect, though generally the backgrounds are left white, as preferred by the Dominican Bromyard.

The white space forms an essential part of the composition, in contrast to the Trinity College Apocalypse where the archaic form of the patterned background is retained.

*   *   *   *

However important colour may be it is the draughtsmanship which makes our artist a real individual, although we do not know his name. The similarities between the Douce Apocalypse and the Westminster panel are striking indeed and closer than anything which can be found to support M. R. James's belief in a connection between this manuscript and Canterbury; yet a practical artist might doubt whether, as has been suggested, the draughtsmen were identical, for the Westminster panel has a curious formal treatment of the nostrils absent in the Douce Apocalypse, and though the Westminster fingers may appear boneless they are not the ultra long, double-jointed fingers of the Douce Apocalypse. Miss O. E. Saunders recognized an Apocalypse from the same *atelier* in the Bibliothèque Nationale of which M. R. James declared that he had 'never seen any other book which struck him as being by the same hand as the Douce Apocalypse' and after his famous Schweich lectures were delivered photographs made him unable to believe it to be the work of another artist. An artist, however, while seeing the obvious resemblances might be less certain, though it is quite clear both came from the same workshop. Analogies between the Douce Apocalypse and the Paris manuscript are so striking that it is certainly impossible not to assume either that one artist copied the other, or that both have a common source—the latter being the most likely as the words of the two manuscripts are certainly copied from a source common to both. On the whole, the drawing, like the script, of the Douce manuscript seems the more refined, and it is interesting to note that some of the more strikingly analogous figures are 'mirror images', as are some of the most similar designs. The tall bearded figure in draperies of classic fall, on p. 11 of the Douce manuscript and p.6 in that of Paris, is a striking case in point. In draperies, hair dressing and facial type the two are remarkably similar—except that they are mirror images. The same is true of the first illustrated design in each series, when the overall arrangement of the Paris manuscript is a mirror image of the Douce design, but where there are differences as well as notable similarities in detail. Thus, the island with the archer drawing his bow in the Douce manuscript's 'insula Garmosia' is paralleled in the Paris manuscript, which contains a motif similar in every way except that the ears of the hare are longer. The tree in each is suitably similar in general design, but there are differences in treatment—that of the Douce being recognizably an oak, with acorns, that of Paris being more formal and decorative and adorned with a bird. The leaves of the Douce tree are uniform in tone, the acorns, with their characteristic 'tips' beautifully observed. The Paris tree, so similar in general structure, is painted in a formal counterchange of light and dark leaves, and the fruit consists of groups of three round forms of no certain character. Moreover, although the total general design is in mirror image, the Paris angel flies towards the saint and whispers in his ear as he flies, but in the Douce picture the angel has alighted behind the saint and has woken him up. One is tempted to see in these phenomena, the use of some method of copying by tracing, since it is unnecessarily difficult to make a straightforward copy in reverse. Or perhaps the common source could have been placed in such a position that one of the copyists took his image from the reverse side of the transparent vellum whilst another faced the original. When light shines through vellum it is quite thin enough to show a clear image from the other side, but it is, of course, seen in reverse. There does indeed exist a drawing of Christ among the candlesticks on transparent vellum on which a note was made that nothing more was to be written upon as it could be better seen if held up to the light.[26] Some of the pages in the Douce manuscript are marred by the appearance of irrelevant dark patches showing through from the back, and the pictures of the common pattern book must have had nothing on their backs.

The artist of the Douce Apocalypse lived at a time when the writings of Albertus Magnus (c. 1250–75) and carved capitals at Rheims (c. 1250–60) were expressing an interest in nature which found supreme expression at Southwell (in the work on the Chapter House capitals) at the end of the century.[27] He was at that special stage of development which occurs in highly skilled and well-trained persons, not deficient in natural observation, who have not had the benefit of the direct study from nature, reckoned obligatory until recently for the artist, since the discoveries of the Renaissance. Thus, in accord with the late thirteenth-century tendency towards naturalism on both sides of the Channel, the vine and the English oak are readily recognizable—though one vine[28] does bear a single oak leaf—as if the artist had started an oak tree and changed his mind; but a botanist would be hard put to it to name the formal sprigs of flowering plants and the artist had not studied locusts.[29] At the same time, carefully executed ears often spring closer to the cheeks than their normal position behind the jaw-line, and the horse—our artist was no horseman—have smooth fleshy tails which later break into hair—halfway to the tufted tails of lions and cows. At one point[30] a tree, forgetful of its place in Gothic art, branches into an attractive plaiting of interlaced boughs, reminiscent of Celtic strapwork. The artist's method of designing trees is made quite clear from the uncoloured drawings where the masses of verdure are indicated in many cases by their external shape only: but on p. 72 there are tree drawings at two stages of development, two trees having their leaves defined by drawing, and two others merely having the general outline of the mass sketched in. On p. 75 three trees are drawn, having the main masses of verdure drawn, and painted (two trees are green, with the trunks not yet coloured, the third is beige all over). Evidently this was the usual practice of the artist—to draw in the main masses of the tree, then apply colour, and lastly (but not on p. 72) to draw in the leaves and further details and to add any last touches of colour—and a strong argument may be made from this method of work that draughtsman and colourist were one. The artist did not seriously attempt a consistently naturalistic treatment of the leaves of his trees on all occasions. On p. 76 for instance a tree bearing three masses of verdure has oak leaves in the central portion, whilst those on either side of it are filled in with a 'fish scale' effect, and p. 85 has a tree against the darkness of the ground which is a design of delicate trefoil shapes in light colour—a treatment similar to that which the Douce painter gives to other plants against a background of rock or meadow, but not elsewhere to trees. The draughtsman of the Trinity College Apocalypse makes no attempt to render his highly stylized trees as recognizable species, his only concession to naturalism being to colour them green.

Birds are well drawn, as they often are in English art, and the wings of the angels are beautiful. Our artist uses commonplace conventions such as the portrayal of clouds with vandyked edges. Fashion of costume (p. 51) is of the second half of the thirteenth century; and architectural details, in the carefully differentiated seven churches of Asia (p. 2), reflect the architecture of the thirteenth and preceding centuries with never an ogee arch to herald the fourteenth-century Decorated style. The artist's ships, like those in the Dublin Apocalypse, have short planking. In one especially pleasing page (p. 23) he manages to get every variety of pose out of each of seven angels with trumpets—the first angel blows his horn (for here are curved horns rather than the straight trumpets demanded more strictly by the text) and some of the others watch him, while others appear to turn away to discuss the note he plays. The master of the Douce Apocalypse, with studied and rather 'French' elegance, follows the fashions in faces and proportions of the courtly in his day—the bulge of the forehead, followed by a curious concave line of eye and cheek such as one sees in thirteenth-century sculptured angels in the latest bays of the Angel Choir at Lincoln, in contrast to the round wide-eyed and delicately modelled faces of St. Albans. He likewise affects the elegant and physically difficult projection of one finger stiffly forward, when the rest are closed over reins or sword hilt, which may almost be likened to the nineteenth-century genteel curling of the little finger over the tea-cup handle. The standing figures curve and sway in the stance sometimes said to be related to the curve of an ivory tusk, medium used for small and precious statues. The Gothic linear patterns of his rich and ample draperies contrast with the soft and clinging draperies of St. Albans and share with Parisian illumination the deep plastic style of late thirteenth-century sculpture where, as Miss Margaret Rickert observes, drapery tends to stand out in stiff, deeply and sharply undercut edges in contrast to the rather Italian heavy classical drapery of the Westminster panel with its deep broad folds. Indeed, our artist's broad treatment and noble compositions inevitably suggest wall-painting especially when they are enlarged from a slide or a film onto a wall. Their unfaded and unrestored colours then indeed give some idea of the appearance of the wall paintings which were executed for Edward I in the decades following his accession, by such leading royal artists as Master Walter of Durham.

Professor Tristram was struck by resemblances between the Douce Apocalypse and the *Estoire de Saint Aedward le Rei*. The latter has been reproduced in facsimile and has been assigned to the most talented follower of Matthew Paris. Both are executed with extreme delicacy of drawing, but lack identity of mannerisms. Thus the attitudes of the characters in the Life of St. Edward are, except in the battle scenes, notable for unvaried upright poses in which the arms alone show dramatic action. In the Douce Apocalypse the design is varied by wildly dramatic poses of the whole body—though of course the text gives warrant for this Baroque sense of movement. The architecture in the Edward book shows an unvarying series of Romanesque forms, in the Douce book the Gothic arch appears, together with Romanesque and fanciful openings. The trees in the Edward Life are—with the exception of one recognizable oak—purely decorative, whereas the Douce book, as suggested above, makes an almost consistent attempt at a decorative treatment of recognizable trees. The Edward artist draws his

15   [continued on p. 32

PLATE 1

GOD'S ANGEL COMES TO JOHN ON PATMOS (MS. page 1)

'The Revelation of Jesus Christ which God gave unto him, to shew unto his servants things which must shortly come to pass; and he sent and signified it by his angel unto his servant John: who bare record of the word of God, and of the testimony of Jesus Christ, and of all things that he saw. Blessed is he that readeth, and they that hear the words of this prophecy, and keep those things which are written therein: for the time is at hand.'—*Revelation*, i, 1–3.

The commentary of Berengaudus says that St. John the Evangelist is the author although some say it was written by another. As this book tells things present and things past as well as things to come why does Christ bid shew unto His servants only things which must come to pass? It is because we can see what is happening and hear what has happened easily, but the future can only be known by the teaching of Scripture and the revelation of God.

Around the island of Patmos ('Cest le hysle de Pathmos') is the sea ('Cest la mer de Bosforum'). It is full of fish and there is a dog on top of a boat. Various islands are shown with their names, a characteristic of the group of manuscripts which M. R. James assigned to Canterbury. On one of them a man is drawing his bow at a hare. This is the second hare to be shown in this manuscript for two hounds are coursing one in the lower margin of the opening page of an Anglo-Norman translation of the Apocalypse which precedes this illus-trated Latin Apocalypse. These animals are wrongly described as rabbits by M. R. James. The point is of some importance in the history of agriculture and the skin trade, for if these were rabbits it would push back by the space of a generation the first advent of these animals in England. The ears are too long for a rabbit, and one only courses hares one does not course rabbits. Notice the steering paddle on the boat—movable rudders first appear in manuscripts a generation or so later.

PLATE 2

LETTER TO PHILADELPHIA (MS. page 9)

'And to the angel of the church in Philadelphia, write, These things saith he that is holy, he that is true, he that hath the key of David, he that openeth, and no man shutteth; and shutteth and no man openeth. I know thy works: behold, I have set before thee an open door, and no man can shut it. . . . Behold, I come quickly: hold that fast which thou hast, that no man take thy crown.'—*Revelation*, iii, 7–8, 11.

St. John is writing in a book with ruled margins, like the Douce Apocalypse itself. On the ground are his ink pot and case. The key of David, applied to Christ in the commentary of Berengaudus, is in the sky. The open door is on the left. The angel is holding that which he has in both hands. Note the transitional style in the arcading of the Church of Philadelphia, both round and pointed arches occurring.

Cest le hyfle de pathmos.

Insula ....

Cest la mer de voffonun.

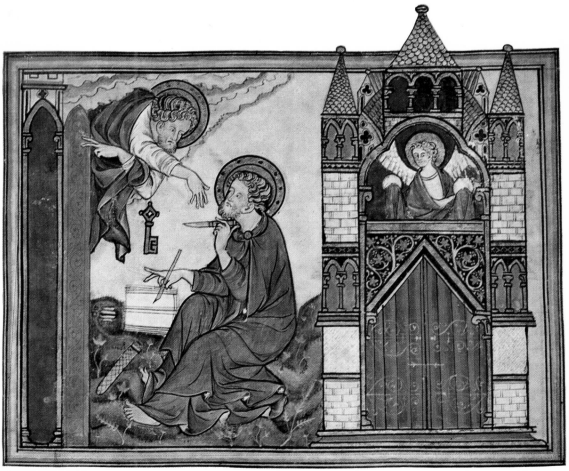

PLATE 3

THE LAMB OPENS THE FIRST SEAL (MS. page 13)

'And I saw when the Lamb opened one of the seven seals, and I heard, as it were the noise of thunder, one of the four beasts, saying, Come, and see. And I saw, and behold, a white horse; and he that sat on him had a bow, and a crown was given unto him, and he went forth conquering, and to conquer.'—*Revelation*, vi, 1–2.

This is the first of six successive pictures in which the Lamb is seen in a cloud in Heaven opening a seal. It is the first of four successive pictures in which St. John is shown on the left of the picture watching a Horseman. In each he is addressed by one of the four beasts described in *Revelation*, iv, 7–8, as a lion, a calf, a man and an eagle. These come *via* Ezekiel from Assyrian imagery and later symbolize the four Evangelists. Here there is the lion of St. Mark. Notice the horseman's arrow, rough bow and carefully drawn harness.

Berengaudus interprets the first seal as relating to events before the Flood. For him the four beasts here signify the doctors of the Church summoning us to come and see with spiritual understanding. The white horse means those who were just, for their innocence makes them to be called white, in the time before the Flood. The rider is the Lord. On succeeding pages Berengaudus discusses the colour symbolism of the red and black horses.

PLATE 4

THE SIXTH SEAL (MS. page 18)

'And I beheld when he had opened the sixth seal, and lo, there was a great earthquake, and the sun became black as sackcloth of hair, and the moon became as blood; and the stars of heaven fell unto the earth, even as a figtree casteth her untimely figs when she is shaken of a mighty wind. And the heaven departed as a scroll when it is rolled together; and every mountain and island were moved out of their places. And the kings of the earth, and the great men, and the rich men, and the chief captains, and the mighty men, and every bondman, and every free man hid themselves in the dens, and in the rocks of the mountains. And said to the mountains and rocks, Fall on us, and hide us from the face of him that sitteth on the throne, and from the wrath of the Lamb: for the great day of his wrath is come, and who shall be able to stand?'—*Revelation*, vi, 12–17.

Berengaudus says that this relates to the destruction of the Jews and to the call of the Gentiles, about which he says that Christ says much in parables.

The falling stars are not shown.

PLATE 5

THE ANGELS AND THE WINDS (MS. page 19)

'And after these things I saw four angels standing on the four corners of the earth, holding the four winds of the earth, that the wind should not blow on the earth, nor on the sea, nor on any tree. And I saw another angel ascending from the east, having the seal of the living God: and he cried with a loud voice to the four angels, to whom it was given to hurt the earth and the sea, saying, Hurt not the earth, neither the sea, nor the trees, till we have sealed the servants of our God in their foreheads. And I heard the number of them that were sealed: and there were sealed an hundred and forty and four thousand of all the tribes of the children of Israel. Of the tribe of Judah were sealed twelve thousand. Of the tribe of Reuben were sealed twelve thousand. Of the tribe of Gad were sealed twelve thousand. . . .'—*Revelation*, vii, 1–5.

The figure appearing from the cloud in the top right-hand corner has a cruciform halo. This type of halo is the mark or sign that an artist is portraying Christ or God the Father, 'for he that hath seen me hath seen the Father also'. Here, however, St. John's words show that an angel is intended, but an angel 'having the seal of the living God'. The word used in the *Vulgate* for a seal is *signum* and the *signum* of the living God is a cruciform halo.

On the left is the globe and on it is the earth, with its four corners. Note the sheep, the buildings, the trees, the fish and the ships. St. John is seated and is holding in his right hand a staff shaped like a T. M. R. James wrongly says he is reading. The book in his left hand is closed and the fore-edge is away from him. The four angels have their hands in front of the mouths of the four winds. Each wind is represented as a face with swollen cheeks between two wings.

PLATE 6

THE FIRST TRUMPET (MS. page 23)

'And the seven angels which had the seven trumpets, prepared themselves to sound. The first angel sounded, and there followed hail and fire mingled with blood, and they were cast upon the earth: and the third part of trees was burnt up, and all green grass was burnt up.'—*Revelation*, v, 6–7.

In this and in five later pictures angels are seen blowing long curved horns. Berengaudus interprets the seven trumpets, unlike the subsequent seven vials, in a good sense. The fire is the Holy Spirit and the blood is Christ. The hail is the speech of the saints striking the hearts of the wicked. The third part of the earth means the saved, in whom everything evil is consumed by the fear and love of God. The trees are the great ones among them. Note the variety in the poses of the angels in this delightful picture, jewel-like with texture enrichments on the right-hand background. The painter of the Trinity College Apocalypse also makes play with textures, brushing on green and sepia over a green wash to suggest the irregularity of earth and grass in odd contrast to the formal patterning of his backgrounds.

PLATE 7
THE FOURTH TRUMPET (MS. page 26)

'And the fourth angel sounded, and the third part of the sun was smitten, and the third part of the moon, and the third part of the stars; so as the third part of them was darkened, and the day shone not for a third part of it, and the night likewise.'—*Revelation*, viii, 12.

M. R. James strangely comments that the human face of the moon is accompanied by a dark crescent and the sun by a dark rim. Actually the crescent and the flames of the sun are not darkened, as might have been expected, but have shadows behind them. The stars are not shown.

Berengaudus interprets the sun as the Jewish people and the moon as the Synagogue, while the stars are the chief priests. Their conversion makes them darkened in the opinion of bad Jews but glorious in the sight of God. They seem dark on account of the real light which is Christ whom they have received.

Notice the grass on the sky-line, drawn with the surprising naturalism that occurs from time to time in early Herbals, which contain some pictures of plants taken from nature among numbers derived from early pictures. Grass rendered with sketchy upright strokes occurs in the very similar Apocalypse manuscript at Paris, mentioned above on p. 13.

PLATE 8
THE HORSEMEN (MS. page 31)

'And thus I saw the horses in the vision, and them that sat on them, having breastplates of fire, and of jacinth, and brimstone: and the heads of the horses were as the heads of lions; and out of their mouths issued fire and smoke and brimstone. By these three was the third part of men killed, by the fire and by the smoke, and by the brimstone, which issued out of their mouths. For their power is in their mouth, and in their tails: for their tails were like unto serpents, and had heads, and with them they do hurt. And the rest of the men which were not killed by these plagues yet repented not of the works of their hands, . . . '—*Revelation*, ix, 17–21.

Berengaudus explains that the horses are the raving people and those who sit upon them are the magnates. The breast plates are the hardness of their hearts which do not allow the sword of the spirit that is the word of God to reach their hearts. The brimstone means their blasphemies.

Silver, used here for mail, occurs on some other pages.

The banner[31] bears a lion rampant with a forked tail. M. R. James rejected the suggestion that this alludes to Simon de Montfort whose arms these are. Montfort's forked lion stood on a red ground not yellow. Yellow was the colour not only of brimstone but, traditionally, of the coat of Judas; while, as Dante explains, red is the colour of faith. The Lord Edward, who routed the host of Montfort, might have approved of what M. R. James here calls playing tricks with the tinctures. James wrongly says the lion is here azure; in fact it is black, the colour of Hell not Heaven. On the death of Edward I his knights lamented one under whose leadership 'we plucked the Kingdom of England from the mouth of the lion, when we freed Daniel, King Henry III, from the hand of the beast in the war of Evesham'.[32]

22

PLATE 9

THE TEMPLE OPENED IN HEAVEN (MS. page 41)

'And the temple of God was opened in heaven, and there was seen in his temple the ark of his testament: and there were lightnings, and voices, and thunderings, and an earthquake, and great hail.'—*Revelation*, xi, 19.

St. John with his book stands contemplating the appearance in Heaven of the Temple. At each end it has triple lancets. Within is a shrine within a thirteenth-century trefoil arch. The Temple is in a cloud in which there are ten human faces and the heads of five creatures with open mouths vomiting forth rays of tempestuous fire upon the earth against a background of hail. On the ground the earthquake has uprooted various plants including three oak trees.

The commentary of Berengaudus says that the Temple can be understood as the Blessed Mary and that the ark is Christ who assumed flesh from Her. The Temple is said to be opened because through Her the Lord is made visible to us. The Temple can also be taken as meaning the Old Testament and the ark as the inner meanings therein about Christ which were revealed to the faithful in Him when He came in the flesh. The lightnings signify His miracles, the voices His preaching. The hailstones are the threats which are often found in the Gospels to shake the hearts of the wicked that they may turn from their iniquity. This commentary is given in the text written in the lower half of p. 41.

PLATE 10

THE NEW SONG (MS. page 54)

'And I looked, and lo, a Lamb stood on the mount Sion, and with him an hundred forty and four thousand, having his Father's name written in their foreheads. And I heard a voice from heaven, as the voice of many waters, and as the voice of a great thunder: and I heard the voice of harpers harping with their harps: and they sung as it were a new song before the throne, and before the four beasts, and the elders: and no man could learn that song but the hundred and forty and four thousand, which were redeemed from the earth.'—*Revelation*, xiv, 1–3.

St. John stands watching in a tall compartment on the left. The four Gospel beasts surround the throne and in compartments each side are six faces in the clouds vomiting fire. Below sit two groups, each of six Elders. At the bottom twelve elders, half with harps, are arranged each side of a quatrefoil containing the Lamb and surmounted by two angels.

PLATE 11

THE VINTAGE AND WINEPRESS OF THE WRATH OF GOD
(MS. page 58)

'And another angel came out of the temple which is in heaven, he also having a sharp sickle. And another angel came out from the altar, which had power over fire; and cried with a loud cry to him that had the sharp sickle, saying, Thrust in thy sharp sickle, and gather the clusters of the vine of the earth; for her grapes are fully ripe. And the angel thrust in his sickle into the earth, and gathered the vine of the earth, and cast it into the great winepress of the wrath of God. And the winepress was trodden without the city, and blood came out of the winepress, even unto the horse bridles, by the space of a thousand and six hundred furlongs.'—*Revelation*, xiv, 17–20.

The artist has shown the blood up to the horses' bridles but the actual winepress is not shown. On the left there is an altar. An altar is associated with bread and wine that is blood. The commentary of Berengaudus explains that the temple in heaven signifies the Church as does the altar. He takes the vine here as signifying the wicked.

PLATE 12

MERCHANTS AND MARINERS LAMENT OVER BABYLON
(MS. page 76)

'The merchants . . . which were made rich by her, shall stand afar off for the fear of her torment, weeping and wailing, and saying, Alas, alas that great city, that was clothed in fine linen, and purple and scarlet, and decked with gold, and precious stones, and pearls! For in one hour so great riches is come to nought. And every shipmaster, and all the company in ships, and sailors, and as many as trade by sea, stood afar off, and cried when they saw the smoke of her burning, saying, What city is like unto this great city! And they cast dust on their heads, and cried, weeping and wailing, saying, Alas, alas that great city, wherein were made rich all that had ships in the sea by reason of her costliness! for in one hour is she made desolate. Rejoice over her, thou heaven, and ye holy apostles and prophets; for God hath avenged you on her.'—*Revelation*, xviii, 15–20.

The commentary of Berengaudus interprets the sea as meaning his period. The shipmasters are evil rulers. The sailors and traders are those who despoil the poor. They lament the burning of Babylon because they are themselves Babylonians and they see their own burning.

The washes of colour on this unfinished picture are a valuable demonstration of the colourist's technique. The scrolls of text incorporated in the picture are written in the script used on charters of the last half of the thirteenth century and the first decades of the fourteenth century. The texts read 'Li quel est semblable a cele grant cyte.' and 'Allas allas i cele grant cyte en ki tuz ki auoient nefs en la mer sunt fet riches de ses pris kar a vn hour'.

26

l'quiet est semblable
N'alcygrate core

Anas Allat icele grante ayra en
se tuz bz duoient nose en la mer
sute fes riebet de sef puist ker a un bruz

PLATE 13

THE FIFTH VIAL OF WRATH (MS. page 66)

'And the fifth angel poured out his vial upon the seat of the beast; and his kingdom was full of darkness; and they gnawed their tongues for pain. And blasphemed the God of Heaven because of their pains and their sores, and did no penance for their deeds.'—*Revelation*, xvi, 10–11.

The commentary of Berengaudus explains that the fifth angel signifies the orthodox in their fight against heretics. Like the locusts, the seat of the beast signifies the heretics; and this is apt because the devil dwells within their hearts. The kingdom is made full of darkness because the Fathers of the Church show how wretched and dark is that teaching of the heretics which had appeared to be bright. They gnaw their tongues because one heretic refutes the errors of another. They blaspheme God because the more they are refuted by the Catholics the more blasphemous they become. They did no penance because hardly any of the inventors of heresy have in fact done penance for their errors.

The Authorized Version reads 'repented not' instead of 'did not penance' ('egerunt penitenciam'). At the beginning of the manuscript text, 'Et quintus angelus', the scribe has left out the initial *E* and has left a square space two lines in height for the insertion of a capital by the rubricator. The initial capital is omitted underneath every picture in the book. A similar space is left on every page, except p. 1, where the empty square is five lines high, and on p. 2, where it is omitted in error. At the end of the gloss the scribe explains that he is re-writing part of the text because there is not enough commentary. He accordingly fills the last four and a half lines with a repetition of verse 10. The beast's chair has wicker sides, turned knobs and a back decorated with three romanesque arches. No colour has been applied on this page. The ruling on this page is typical of all the other pages, except the last one (p. 97) on which it is red. The reproduction is the size of the original.

t quintus angelus effud
phialam suam super sedem
bestie er factum est regnum eius
tenebrosum er commanducauerir
linguas pre dolore suas. er blas
phemauerunt deum celi pre dolo
ribus er uulneribus suis. er non
egerunt penitenciam ex operibz
suis. // Quintus angelus herodoxos panc
qui contra hereticos dimicauerint
significat. quemadmodum t illum diximus sig
nificasse qui in superiori uisione. quintus tuba
cecinit. er sicut ille per laudeas hereci delignan
sunt: ita er hic per sedem bestie heretici delignatur.
Bestia autem diabolum significat. Iure igitur he
retici sedes bestie dicuntur. quia in eorum cordib;
diabolus inhabitat. Quintus igitur angelus ef
fudit phialam suam super sedem bestie. quia sac
ti uiri errores hereticorum urgentes que pena sit
iniustitie manifestare studuerint. factum est illo
regnum eius tenebrosum. quia illis quib; doce

na hereticorum falsissa indehirur: per doctrinam sco
rum patrum. q; misera er tenebrosa. cet demonstra
uun est. Commanducauerint linguas suas pre do
loribus. quia singulis singulorum cruces apostolb
bant. Nam neq; artus serinis cnmonium ill'sa
bestium ill quemquam Morum neq; illi illum.
S; unusquisq; heresim suam stabilit uolens: er
rorum errores reprehendebat. Qui etiam deum pre
doloribz t uulneribz suis blasphemasse dicuntur. t
Videbitur quippe heretici a catholicis uiris semper
conuincerentur. Vulnera eorum erant errores sin
gulorum. Blasphemabunt uero heretici deum pre
doloribz suis. quia quanto amplius a catholicis ui
ris superabantur. tanto ampliores blasphemias ad
uos uincendos inuenebant. Inpellebant michilo
minius eos ad deum blasphemandum inter quos y
scebantur. qui etiam sine penitencia fuisse dicuntur.
Vix enim aliquem ex interioribz heresum inuen
uos qui penitenciam egerir in suis erroribus. er cete
Rescribitur hic textus
pro textu glose. zc. // Er quintus an
gelus effudit phialam suam t
super sedem bestie er factum est
regnum eius tenebrosum er co
manducauerint linguas suas.

PLATE 14

CHRIST BLESSING THOSE WHO HAVE EARNED
THE TREE OF LIFE AND THE NEW JERUSALEM
AND REJECTING THE WICKED (MS. page 96)

'I am Alpha and Omega, the beginning and the end, the first and the last. Blessed are they that wash their robes in the blood of the Lamb that have power in the Tree of Life and enter the City by the gates. For without are dogs, and sorcerers, and whoremongers, and murderers, and idolaters, and whoever loveth and maketh a lie.'—*Revelation*, xxii, 13–15.

Notice the contrasting gestures of Christ's right and left hands to indicate acceptance of those at his right hand and rejection of those at his left, whose idol has fallen right out of the picture, whither the dogs are going, away from Christ. Underneath Christ four naked figures are washing their robes. The Authorized Version says 'Blessed are they that do his command-ments' and nothing about the washing of robes which comes at this point in the *Vulgate*. M. R. James failed to understand why the figures seemed to be 'eagerly taking white garments out of tombs?'.[33] The script above the wicked reads 'De fors les chens et les venimous et les nient chastes et les omicides et ke seruent as maumez'. The last word, 'Mahomets', means idols. There is an attempt at perspective in the drawing of the crenellations of the Heavenly City. One of the robes is being held in such a way that the cut of the neck is very clearly displayed.

The commentary of Berengaudus interprets the robes as our souls and the Tree of Life as wisdom. The power is the power to root out vices and to do good works. The gate is that of which the Gospel says 'I am the door: by me if any man enter in, he shall be saved' (*John*, x, 9).

At the beginning of the manuscript text, 'Ego sum alfa', the scribe has left out the initial *E*, as on plate 13, and left a square space two lines in height for the insertion of a capital by the rubricator, as on plate 13. Gold has been applied to the relevant parts of this page. There is green on the ground in the bottom right-hand corner and in details elsewhere.

go sum alfa 7o. primus et
notissimus. principium 7
finis. beati qui lauant stolas suas
ut sit potestas illis in ligno uite
er p portas intrent in ciuitatem.
Foris canes 7 uenefici et impudi
ce homicide et idolis seruientes. et
omnis qui amat mendacium. et
facit. // Ego sum alpha 7 o. pri
mus 7 nouissimus. principium
et finis 7c. Possumus per stolas in
hoc loco animas nostras intelligere 7 qa
assidue peccamus necesse est ut stolas. idem
animas orando. uigilando. ieiunando. ele
mosinas largiendo. assidue lauemus per

lignum uite possumus sapienciam intel
ligere. dicente salomone. lignum uite est
his qui apprehenderint eam. 7 qui tenuerit
eam beatus. Potestatem in ligno uite. id
est in sapiencia habent sancti. qr cumque sa
piencia possidet potens est ad omnia uicia
extirpanda. ad temptationes demonum de
uincendas 7 ad omnia bona opera peragen
da. Sicut dicit salomon. Melior est
paciens uiro forti 7 qui dominatur animo
suo expugnatore urbium. Valent er
go per portas intrant in ciuitate. p illam
scilicet portam que dicit in euangelio. 7
Ego ostium per me si quis introierit sal
uabitur 7 ingredietur. 7 egredietur. 7c.

drapery with some little fretful touches reminiscent here and there of much earlier Romanesque types, the Douce MS. drapery falls in simpler, calmer folds. In short, the resemblances between the two might possibly arise if one artist had drawn the Edward pictures at the beginning of his life and those of the Douce Apocalypse when his style had matured and after he had had time to shed archaisms of drapery treatment and to gain his mannered treatment of the hands. The unfinished pages reveal the artist's full delicacy of line. Mastery of line is an English characteristic, but some of these pages call to mind the sensitive touch of Botticelli.

REFERENCES

[1] Reproduced as the frontispiece of M. R. James, *The Apocalypse in Latin and French (Bodleian MS. Douce* 180), Roxburghe Club 1922. The bindings of this volume are incorrectly lettered 'The Douce Apocalypse (Bodl. MS. 180).' James wrongly describes a hare being coursed by a hound at the foot of the page as a rabbit (*id.*, p. 7, cf. p. 22 where another hare is called a rabbit). See p. 16.

[2] *id.*, p. 3.

[3] Printed, Migne, *Patrologia Latina*, vol. 17.

[4] W. Kamlah, *Apocalypse und Geschichtstheologie*, Historische Studien 285, Berlin 1935; he discusses twelfth-century English commentaries on p. 55. A. Wächtel, *Die Weltgeschichtlich Apokalypse-Auslegung des Minoriten Alexander von Bremen*, 1957.

[5] H. Grundman, *Neue Forschungen über Joachim von Fiore. Münsterische Forschungen*, 1950, 48.

[6] M. R. James, *The Dublin Apocalypse*, Roxburghe Club 1932.

[7] M. R. James, *The Apocalypse in Latin, MS. 10 in the Collection of Dyson Perrins, F.S.A.*, Oxford 1927.

[8] L. Delisle and P. Meyer, *L'Apocalypse en Français au xiiie siècle*, Société des anciens textes français, 1901.

[9] Like Bodleian Library, MS. Auct. D.4.17. See *The Apocalypse of St. John the Divine*, Roxburghe Club 1876. Six editions of Apocalypse block-books were modelled on this; Gertrud Bing, 'Apocalypse Block-Books and their Manuscript Models', *Journal of the Warburg and Courtauld Institutes*, v, 1942, 143–58.

[10] *Bodleian Library Record*, V, 283.

[11] *Bodleian Quarterly Record*, VII, 370.

[12] 'To Canterbury, where French influence was very strong, I assign it until I am forced to relinquish that position'; M. R. James, *The Apocalypse in Art*, p. 58.

[13] M. R. James, *The Apocalypse in Latin and French (Bodleian MS. Douce* 180), p. 20.

[14] E. G. Millar, *English Illuminated MSS. from the xth to the xiiith Centuries*, pp. 62–3, plates 93–4.

[15] E. W. Tristram, *English Medieval Wall Painting in the Thirteenth Century*, pp. 89, 102, 108, 121, 129 and 216, and Supplementary plates 8–10.

[16] Francis Wormald, *Paintings in Westminster Abbey and Contemporary Paintings*, Annual Lecture on Aspects of Art, Henriette Hertz Trust, Proceedings of British Academy, 1949.

[17] The reproductions in Tristram and Wormald, *op. cit.*, are more suitable for comparison than those in *Historical Monuments Commission Report, Westminster*.

[18] Wilhelm Neuss, *Die Apokalypse des hl. Johannes in den Altspanischen und Altchristlichen Bibelillustration nebst einem Tafelbande* (Span. Forsch. d. Görresgesellschaft 2 Reihe, Bd. 2, 3), Munster 1931.

[19] H. Wolfflin ed., *Die Bamberger Apokalypse in eine Reichenauer Bilderhandschrift vom Jahre* 1000, Munich 1918.

[20] M. R. James, *The Apocalypse in Art*, The Schweich Lectures of the British Academy 1927, British Academy 1931, pp. 2–20 and prefatory note.

[21] O. E. Saunders, *English Illumination*, Florence 1928, vol. 1, pp. 83–92 and vol. 2, plate 97b.

[22] Brother William, the companion of St. Francis, second in that Order, English by birth; in British Museum, Cotton MS., Nero D.I, fol. 156, reproduced, Peter Brieger, *English Art 1216–1307* (Oxford History of Art), 1957, plate 55b.

[23] Ernst Benz, *Ecclesia Spiritualis Kirchenidee und Geschichtstheologie der Franziskanischen Reformation*, Stuttgart 1934, p. 199.

[24] Alfred Nicholson, *Cimabue, a Critical Study* (Princeton Monographs in Art and Archaeology), 1932, pp. 9–10 and fig. 10.

[25] Peter Brieger, *op. cit.*, p. 99.

[26] *id.*, p. 161.

[27] N. Pevsner, *Leaves of Southwell*, with photographs by F. L. Attenborough, 1943, p. 63. Cf. O. Pächt, 'Early Italian Nature Studies', *Journal of Warburg and Courtauld Institutes*, vol. 13, 1950, pp. 13–47.

[28] MS. Douce 180, p. 27.

[29] MS. Douce 180, p. 28.

[30] MS. Douce 180, p. 27. A floral border on a verso is often a mirror image of a recto in French MSS.

[31] Gereth M. Spriggs points out that this banner is not a pennon as stated by M. R. James, *The Douce Apocalypse*, p. 29. Pennons were pointed and were carried by mere knights. Banners were square and indicated the rank of a leader, as here.

[32] 'Commendatio lamentabilis in transitu magni regis Edwardi' in *Chronicles of the Reigns of Edward I and II* (Rolls Series) 1883, ii, p. 14.

[33] M. R. James, *The Douce Apocalypse*, p. 45.